MEN-AT-ARMS SERIES

EDITOR: MARTIN WINDROW

# Napoleon's Marshals

*Text by* EMIR BUKHARI

*Colour plates by* CHRIS WARNER

OSPREY PUBLISHING LONDON

Published in 1979 by
Osprey Publishing Ltd
Member company of the George Philip Group
12–14 Long Acre, London WC2E 9LP
© Copyright 1979 Osprey Publishing Ltd

ISBN 0 85045 305 4

Filmset by BAS Printers Limited,
Over Wallop, Hampshire
Printed in Hong Kong

The author would like to express his gratitude to the
staffs of the Musée de l'Armée, Paris, and the National
Army Museum, London; Jean and M. le Baron de
Gerlache de Gomery; Caroline Lederer and Chris
Brennan. Particular mention should be made of
Lucien Rousselot's *Armée française*, which provided the
main source material for the illustrations and body
copy on marshals' dress, and Brigadier Peter Young's
*Napoleon's Marshals*, which yielded the majority of the
marshals' biographies.

# The Marshals

*'The history of the marshalate of France is the history of France herself in its most noble aspect.'*

(J. Brunon)

*'Over-accustomed to obeying, [the marshals] lacked a spirit of initiative, and, as early as 1809, they were weary of that obedience while silently cursing their master.'*

(J-C Quennevat)

The rank of Marshal of France was first introduced in 1047 and ran continuously until the Convention, when, with popular feeling being such that the status inherent in the rank went against the grain of Republicanism, it was abolished on 21 February 1793. The next ten years saw the rise to power of Napoleon Bonaparte, who, on 19 May 1804, the day following his proclamation of Empire, resurrected the title in the guise of *Maréchal de l'Empire*.

That same day, the Emperor elevated eighteen *généraux de division* to that rank, among whom were four no longer on the active list (Kellermann, Lefebvre, Pérignon and Sérurier) who were dubbed *honorary* marshals. He later added to that list Victor in 1807; Macdonald, Marmont and Oudinot in 1809; Suchet in 1811; Gouvion Saint Cyr in 1812; Poniatowski in 1813; and Grouchy (to all intents and purposes) in 1815.

Much has been made of their personal rivalries, jealousies, greed and lust for power; but it should be recalled that these men were largely of humble origin and but rarely of any education. They were career soldiers and volunteers long before the *levée en masse* of 1793: men who had lived life in rough company and circumstances, and come a long way in a very short time. They had every soldier's vices and virtues; they were glory-seeking, self-aggrandizing and envious of social status.

Napoleon boasted to the *Conseil d'Etat*: 'Not one of my marshals has the makings of a commander-in-chief', and he was doubtless right (save in the case of his honorary marshals, who had proven their ability as army leaders during the Revolutionary Wars), for that capacity was the last thing he sought from his subordinates. Napoleon's method of command was such that he expected his marshals to obey, not initiate; and he slowly and deliberately set out to ensure that his senior officers became merely blind agents who executed his orders without hesitation, discussion or personal opinion. 'Confine yourself strictly to the orders I shall be sending you: execute my instructions punctually; everyone must hold themselves in readiness and stay at their posts: only I, I alone know what I must do.' The Emperor wrote this to his Chief of Staff, Berthier, on 14 February 1806, and it neatly sums up his whole perspective towards his most senior officers and closest associates.

In such circumstances, it is hardly surprising that the marshals' stifled military ambitions found vent in the accumulation of riches, lands and titles; and these the Emperor was pleased to lavish on them in return for the submission of their wills to his.

The marshals' attitude towards Napoleon in the twilight years after Russia, becomes comprehensible with the appreciation that their loyalty was only of the most servile nature. Lefebvre, a loyal but frank man, spoke for them all when he summed up his last interview with Napoleon prior to the abdication: 'I told him it was time for us to enjoy some rest. Could it be he believes that when we have titles, manors and estates, we will go and get ourselves killed for him? It's as much his own fault: he took the shirts off our backs too early!'

It is rather unlikely that any of the marshals was capable of conceiving and executing an overall campaign strategy which would dictate the manoeuvres and tactics of an army at best advantage against the enemy at a given battle. But in the midst of battle itself they performed as exceptional leaders of men. In the section that follows, the war record of each and every marshal speaks for itself. These are 'potted' biographies in chronological and alphabetical order; they are of necessity in abbreviated form, however. Sadly, they do not permit us to see Ney, already dubbed 'the bravest of the brave' by his soldiers, so stupefy the Emperor with his courage that he exclaimed 'C'est un Lion!'; or 'Old' Masséna, the last man to take sanctuary on the island of Lobau, leaving behind not a single wounded man, after the bloody battle of Essling; or Davout stagger from his stretcher with a gaping stomach wound to lead his troops afresh into the mêlée at Borodino; or Murat grabbing the colonel who ordered the retreat at Semenovskoye by the scruff of the neck and asserting 'Eh! J'y-reste bien moi!'; or Lannes with a scaling ladder before the walls of Ratisbonne, rushing forward into the breach with his grenadiers. . . .

## Biographies

### AUGEREAU

Pierre-François-Charles Augereau, *Duc de Castiglione*, 1757–1816.

1804: Became a Marshal of France and commanded the Brest invasion camp.

1805: Awarded the Grand Eagle of the Legion of Honour and, 30 August, appointed commander of the VII Corps of the *Grande Armée*. Fought at Feldkirch.

1806: Engaged at Jena and Kolozomb.

1807: Wounded at the battle of Eylau.

1808: Became the Duke of Castiglione, 19 March.

1809: Appointed commander of the VII Corps of the *Armée d'Espagne*, 1 June, and received surrender of Gerona, 10 December.

1810–13: Held various posts in Germany and commanded the IX Corps at Naumberg and Leipzig.

1814: Made Commander-in-Chief of the Army of the East (or of the Rhône), 5 January,

and fought at Saint-Georges, 18 March. Forsook the Emperor in April and, upon the restoration of the Bourbons, became a *Chevalier de Saint-Louis*, 21 June.

1815: Struck from the roll of Marshals by the returned Emperor, 10 April. Following the Hundred Days campaign he was appointed to the Council of War to try Marshal Ney, but, the Council declaring itself incompetent to judge the case, was retired in disgrace.

Pierre-François-Charles AUGEREAU, 1757–1816. Son of a domestic servant and fruiterer, Augereau was basically an adventurer who had done rather well for himself. Greedy, rapacious and an opportunist of the first order, he was a spirited man whose main claim to fame lay in his steadfastness at the battle of Castiglione in 1796, for which Napoleon gave him full credit (which was something of a novelty for the Emperor). He is shown in full ceremonial dress. (Engr. Johnson. Author's Collection)

# BERNADOTTE

Jean-Baptiste-Jules Bernadotte, *Prince de Pontecorvo*, King of Sweden, 1763–1844.

1804: Became Governor of Hanover, 14 May, and a Marshal of France.

1805: Awarded the Grand Eagle of the Legion of Honour, 2 February. Commanded the I Corps of the the *Grande Armée* and fought at Ulm and Austerlitz.

1806: Became Prince of Pontecorvo, 5 June, and Grand Dignitary of the order of the *Couronne de Fer* of Lombardy. Present at the battles of Jena-Auerstädt, but fought at Halle, Nossentin, Crivitz, Lübeck and Schwartau.

1807: Fought at Mohrüngen and wounded at the River Passarge action and at Spanden, following which he was compelled to give up his command. Made Governor of the Hanseatic Cities, 14 July.

1808: Occupied Jutland and Fünen, and awarded the Order of the Elephant of Denmark.

1809: Given command of the Saxon Army, 7 March, which became the IX Corps of the *Grande Armée*, 8 April. Grossly mishandled his corps at Wagram, and was instantly dismissed. Returned to Paris, 30 July, where he was appointed to command the army assembled on the River Escaut (Scheldt) to oppose the British Walcheren landing, 12 August. Piqued by a proclamation which Bernadotte made to his troops, Napoleon summoned him to Vienna, where he again dismissed him. Relinquished his command, 24 September.

1810: 21 August, elected Crown Prince of Sweden by the Swedish States-General. Adopted by King Charles XIII on 5 November.

1812: Following Napoleon's invasion of Swedish Pomerania, the Crown Prince allied himself with the Tsar of Russia.

1813: Brought Sweden into the Sixth Coalition against France and fought at Grossbeeren, Dennewitz and Leipzig. Invaded Holstein and compelled Denmark

Jean-Baptiste-Jules **BERNADOTTE, 1763–1844.** Bernadotte was a firm, resolute and very capable man who is frequently maligned for declaring war on France in 1813. He had been adopted by the King of Sweden, Charles XIII, in 1810, and, as Crown Prince, took his rôle seriously, leaving behind his identity as a French general and adopting that of a future head of state. When Napoleon invaded Swedish Pomerania in 1812, Bernadotte concluded an armistice with the Tsar of Russia, who ceded him Norway, and in the following year joined the Sixth Coalition against France. Became Charles XIV of Sweden in 1818, from whom the present royal family is descended. **(Engr. after Kinson. Author's Collection)**

to cede Norway to Sweden by the Treaty of Kiel, 14 January 1814.

## BERTHIER

Louis-Alexandre Berthier, *Prince de Neuchâtel et Valengin, Prince de Wagram*, 1753–1815.

1799–1807: Minister of War and Chief of Staff to Napoleon and then the *Grande Armée*.

1808: Chief of Staff to the *Armée d'Espagne* and then became *Major-Général* of the *Grande Armée*.

1809: Temporary Commander-in-Chief of the *Armée d'Allemagne*.

1810–14: Chief of Staff to the *Grande Armée*. Following abdication, became *capitaine* of the *5eme Cie. du Garde du Corps Royale*, 1 June, a peer of France, 4 June, and a commander of *Saint-Louis*, 25 September.

1815: Escorted Louis XVIII to Ghent at beginning of Hundred Days, then retired to Bamberg, where he died, falling from a window in unknown circumstances on 1 June.

## BESSIERES

Jean-Baptiste Bessières, *Duc d'Istrie*, 1768–1813.

1804: Became a Marshal of France, 19 May, Grand Officer of the Legion of Honour and commander of its 3rd Cohort, 14 June, and then *Colonel-Général* of the cavalry of the Imperial Guard, 20 July.

1805: Awarded the Grand Eagle of the Legion of Honour and became Commander of the Order of the *Couronne de Fer* (of Lombardy), 2 February. Fought at Austerlitz.

1806: Fought at Jena and Biezun.

1807: Fought at Eylau and Friedland. Awarded the Grand Cross of the Order of St Henry of Saxony, the Grand Cross of Christ of Portugal and the Golden Eagle of Württemberg. Became Ambassador to Württemberg.

1808: Appointed commander of the *Corps d'Observation des Pyrénées Occidentales*, 19 March, and fought at Medina del Rio Seco, 14 July, and Burgos, following which he entered Madrid with King Joseph. Commanded the II Corps then the Reserve Cavalry of the *Armée d'Espagne*, 9 November, and fought at Somosierra, Madrid and Guadalajara.

1809: Recalled to Paris, 9 March, then appointed commander of the Reserve Cavalry of the *Grande Armée* and fought at Landshut, Neumarkt, Ebersberg, Essling and Wagram. Became Duke of Istria, 28 May, and then replaced Bernadotte as

Louis-Alexandre BERTHIER, 1753–1815. Berthier's genius lay in the pen rather than the sword, and his subtle and complex character adapted itself well to the intricacies of staff work. Quick to spot his talents, Bonaparte employed him as his Chief of Staff from the campaign of Italy in 1796 through to the campaign of France in 1814. As Chief of Staff he assumed the staggering burden of providing and collating intelligence reports on countries and armies for the Emperor's information, as well as devising, writing and transmitting Napoleon's strategic concepts in the form of orders of march to each of the army's corps. Died in mysterious circumstances just prior to the Hundred Days campaign, falling from a window in Bamberg. (Eng. Cambert. Author's Collection)

Commander-in-Chief of the *Armée du Nord*. Fought at Flushing.

1810: Appointed commander of the Imperial Guard at Paris, 19 January, then Governor of Strasbourg, 19 March.

1811: Became General-in-Chief of the *Armée du Nord*, 15 January, then served in Spain and fought at Fuentes d'Onoro. Returned to Paris, 20 September.

1812: Appointed commander of the Cavalry of the Imperial Guard for the duration of the Russian campaign.

1813: Appointed commander of the Imperial Guard, 10 April. Killed, 1 May, by a cannonball at Rippach, near Weissenfels, on the eve of the battle of Lützen.

**Jean-Baptiste BESSIERES, 1768–1813.** An old and close friend of the Emperor's, Bessières was a gifted cavalry commander, a mediocre corps commander, but a strong if rather conservative leader of men. As *Colonel-Général* of the Cavalry of the Guard, he is usually depicted wearing the uniform of the *Chasseurs à Cheval*, an option on the regulation marshals' garb he would doubtless have worn for state occasions. He rode into the path of a cannonball, which killed him outright, at Rippach, near Weissenfels, on the eve of the battle of Lützen, 1 May 1813. (Engr. after Le Bel. Author's Collection)

## BRUNE

Guillaume-Marie-Anne Brune, 1763–1815.

1804:   Ambassador to Turkey until 17 December. Became a Marshal of France.

1805:   Invested with the Grand Eagle of the Legion of Honour.

1806:   Became Governor-General of the Hanseatic Cities, 15 December.

1807:   Appointed commander of the *Corps d'Observation* of the *Grande Armée*, 29 April. Following his seizure of the city of Stralsund on 15 July, he fell into disfavour with the Emperor for his wording of the convention he had drawn up with the defeated Swedish Army, and was disgraced.

1814:   Rallied to the monarchy and made a *Chevalier de Saint-Louis*, 1 June.

1815:   Reverted to the Emperor upon his return and became Governor of Provence and commander of the 8th Military Division, in place of Masséna, 11 April, then commander of the *Corps d'Observation du Var*, 17 April. Made a peer of France, 2 June. Occupied Toulon until the end of July when, following a royal order for his arrest, he was murdered by a mob of royalists at Avignon on his way to Paris.

**Guillaume-Marie-Anne BRUNE, 1763–1815.** A brave and efficient soldier, Brune had joined the ranks as late as 1789, forsaking his career as journalist for the National Guard of Paris, after which he enjoyed a meteoric rise to Marshal and Governor of the Hanseatic Cities, 1806. Ironically, he was murdered by a group of ultra-royalists during the *Terreur Blanche*, August 1815, despite the fact that he was one of the Emperor's *persona non grata* generals—disgraced from 1806 to 1814 for graft.

**Louis Nicolas DAVOUT, 1770–1823.** One of the Emperor's most skilled lieutenants, if one of the most universally disliked for his severity and rudeness, Davout was a truly great military leader: meticulous over detail, efficient, firm of character and as brave as a lion. As Minister of War during the Hundred Days campaign, he concluded the armistice with the invading Allied powers on 3 July 1815. We see him in full dress riding uniform. Note the aiguillettes on his right shoulder, signifying his status as *Colonel-Général* of the *Grenadiers à Pied* of the Guard. (Engr. Muller. Author's Collection)

## DAVOUT

Louis Nicholas Davout, *Duc d'Auerstädt, Prince d'Eckmühl*, 1770–1823.

1804:  Commanded the *Camp de Bruges*. Promoted Marshal of France, 19 May, and *Colonel-Général* of the Imperial Guard.

1805:  Awarded the Grand Eagle of the Legion of Honour, 2 June. Appointed commander of the III Corps of the *Grande Armée* and fought at Marienzell and Austerlitz.

1806:  Fought at Jena-Auerstädt and Eylau, where he was severely wounded.

1807:  Appointed Governor-General of the Grand Duchy of Warsaw, 15 July.

1808:  Became Duke of Auerstädt, 28 March, and commanded the *Armée du Rhin*.

1809:  Commanded the III Corps of the *Grande Armée* and fought at Eckmühl and Wagram. Became Prince of Eckmühl, 15 August.

1810–11:  Held various high commands in Germany with headquarters at Hamburg, including commanding the *Corps d'Observation de l'Elbe*.

1812:  Commanded I Corps of the *Grande Armée* during the Russian campaign and fought at Smolensk and Borodino. Led the rearguard of the *Grande Armée* from 19 October to 3 November, and fought at Fedorovskoye. Fought at Krasnoe and the Berezina.

1813:  Defended Dresden, 9 to 19 March, then occupied Hamburg, 30 May, from where he fought at Lauenburg, 18 August.

1814:  Finally surrendered Hamburg, following the Emperor's abdication, on 27 May. Retired to Savigny-sur-Orge and played no part in the First Restoration.

1815:  Became Minister of War, 20 March to 8 July, and a peer of the Empire, 2 June, under the returned Emperor. Defended Paris throughout the Hundred Days campaign, defeating Blücher on 30 June. Finally ceded the city under the Convention of Paris, 3 July, and withdrew his army to the Loire, where, on 14 July, he surrendered to the returned Bourbons. Dismissed from office on 27 July and exiled to Louviers, 27 December.

## GOUVION-SAINT-CYR

Laurent, *Comte puis Marquis de Gouvion-Saint-Cyr*, 1764–1830.

1804:  Became *Colonel-Général* of Cuirassiers, 6 July, while *lieutenant-général* of the *Corps d'Observation du Royaume de Naples*.

1805:  Commanded the *Armée d'Italie* during the

Austrian campaign and fought at Castelfranco. Awarded the Grand Eagle of the Legion of Honour, 2 February.

1806: Appointed Commander-in-Chief of the 1st Reserve Corps (*Camp de Boulogne*), 15 December.

1808: Served in Spain, commanding the VI Corps, and fought at Rosas, Barcelona and Molins del Rey.

1809: Fought at Valls, 25 February, then laid siege to Gerona. Abandoned his command before the arrival of his successor and was recalled to France in disgrace.

1812: Appointed commander of the VII (Bavarian) Corps of the *Grande Armée*, 8 February, and fought at Polotsk, 17 August. Assumed command of the II Corps of the *Grande Armée* in place of Oudinot, 18 August, and completed the wounded Marshal's victory. Became a Marshal of France as a consequence. Wounded at the second battle of Polotsk and resigned his command.

1813: Became military adviser to Prince Eugene, successor to the command of the *Grande Armée* as from 24 January. Assumed command of the XI Corps of the *Grande Armée* in place of Augereau, 16 February, but relieved by Macdonald, 10 March, owing to bad health. Commanded the XIV Corps of the *Grande Armée* in the defence of Dresden, 25 August, and the French centre at the battle, 26 and 27 August. Led the defence of the city from September to 11 November, when he capitulated and was taken prisoner.

1814: Returned to France in June and made a peer of the realm, 4 June.

1815: Appointed commander of the army at Orléans, 19 March, assembled to bar Napoleon's advance. Deserted by his troops in favour of the Emperor, he retired to Bourges, 24 March, and took no part in the Hundred Days campaign save becoming a member of the Council of Defence at Paris. Became Minister of War in place of Davout, 8 July to 25 September.

Laurent, *Comte* and later *Marquis de* **GOUVION SAINT CYR**, **1764–1830.** Something of an eccentric and recluse, Gouvion Saint Cyr was a cautious commander whose advancement proved slow. He was a talented soldier, painter and musician, and a calm and thoughtful commander. The illustration depicts him in *frac* tunic, the marshals' equivalent to the *surtout*. (Vernet. Author's Collection)

**Emmanuel, *Marquis de* GROUCHY, 1766–1847. Commanded the French invasion force against Ireland during the Revolutionary Wars and later developed into one of the finest heavy cavalry leaders of the Empire. Led the *Bataillon Sacré* during the retreat from Moscow. After Waterloo he fled in exile to the United States but later, following the general amnesty of 1821, returned to France.**

## GROUCHY

Emmanuel, *Marquis de Grouchy*, 1766–1847.

1805: Commanded the 2nd Division of the II Corps of the *Grande Armée*, 30 August, and fought at Ulm.

1806: Commanded the 2nd Division of Dragoons of the Reserve Cavalry of the *Grande Armée* and fought at Zehdenick and Prentzlow.

1807: Fought at Eylau and Friedland. Awarded the Grand Cross of the Military Order of Bavaria, 29 June, the Grand Eagle of the Legion of Honour, 13 July, and made a commander of the *Couronne de Fer*.

1808: Commanded the cavalry of the *Armée d'Espagne* and suppressed the 'Dos de Mayo' revolt in Madrid.

1809: Served in Italy, commanding the 1st Dragoon Division under Prince Eugene. Fought at Wagram and succeeded Mar-

mont as *Colonel-Général* of the *Chasseurs à Cheval de la Garde*, 31 July.

1812: Commanded the III Corps of reserve cavalry, 28 January, and wounded at Borodino. Appointed commander of the *Bataillon Sacré* during the retreat.

1813: Took no part in the German campaign through ill-health.

1814: Became Commander-in-Chief of the cavalry of the *Grande Armée* for the campaign of France and fought at Brienne, La Rothière, Vauchamps, Montmirail, Troyes, Braisne and Craonne. Under the First Restoration, appointed inspector-general of *chasseurs* and lancers, 19 July.

1815: Commanded the *Armée du Midi*. Became a Marshal of France, 15 April, and a peer of France, 2 June, under the returned Emperor. Appointed commander of the right wing of the *Armée du Nord*, he fought at Fleurus and Ligny, and then pursued the retreating Prussians, thereby missing Waterloo, but fighting at Gembloux and Wavre. With the Second Restoration, his name was struck from the list of Marshals, 1 August, and he went into exile in America.

## JOURDAN

Jean-Baptiste, *Comte Jourdan*, 1762–1833.

1804: Became a Marshal of the Empire and appointed, 26 January, commander of the *Armée d'Italie*.

1805: Awarded the Grand Eagle of the Legion of Honour. Retained command of the *Armée d'Italie* until 6 September.

1806: Became Governor of Naples and appointed as Chief of Staff to King Joseph.

1808: Became Chief of Staff to the *Armée d'Espagne*, 17 July, and took up his appointment on 22 August.

1809: Replaced Lefebvre as commander of the IV Corps of the *Armée d'Espagne* from 10 January to 21 February. Engaged at Talavera and Almonacid, then returned to France in October.

1811: Became Governor of Madrid, 8 July.

1812: Appointed Chief of Staff to King Joseph, 16 March. Fought at Salamanca and Vittoria, following which he was recalled to France, 12 July.

1813: Retired, 7 August.

1814: Recalled to command the 14th and 15th Military Divisions at Rouen, 30 January. With the return of the Bourbons, he was made a *Chevalier de Saint-Louis*, 2 June, and appointed commander of the 15th Military Division, 21 June.

1815: Upon the return of the Emperor, he became a peer of the Empire, 2 June, then Governor of Besançon and commander of the 6th Military Division, 4 June. After Waterloo, he rallied to the monarchy and presided over the Council of War that condemned Marshal Ney to death.

Jean-Baptiste, *Comte* JOURDAN, 1762–1833. We see the Marshal in full dress riding uniform of a Commander-in-Chief, 1804-07. Jourdan fought under Lafayette in the American War of Independence, and later saw his most distinguished service during the Revolutionary Wars. As a commander, however, he was rather timid and better suited to defensive rather than offensive warfare. Napoleon therefore accorded him only secondary posts, but he found favour and distinction in later years as Governor of *Les Invalides* and Minister for Foreign Affairs under King Louis-Philippe. (Author's Collection)

François-Etienne Christophe KELLERMAN, 1735–1820. Already thirty-four in the year of Napoleon's birth, Kellermann was the oldest of all the marshals, and famous long before the Empire as the victor of Valmy in 1792, for which he was honoured during the course of the Empire with a dukedom. Under the Empire he was charged with the organization of all *dêpots militaires* on French soil, a strictly second-rate appointment; but he was later more actively employed, in 1813, as commander of the *Corps d'Observation du Rhin*.

## KELLERMANN

François-Etienne Christophe Kellermann, *Duc de Valmy*, 1735–1820.

1804: Became a Marshal of France, 19 May.

1805: Awarded the Grand Eagle of the Legion of Honour.

1806: Commander of the III Reserve Corps on the Rhine.

1808: Became Duke of Valmy, 3 June.

1813: Appointed commander of the *Corps d'Observation du Rhin*, 20 January.

1814: Appointed King's Commissioner of the 3rd Military Division in May, then became

Jean LANNES, 1769–1809. Nicknamed the 'French Ajax', Lannes was an intrepid soldier and exceptional commander, though his courage might have got the better of his cool head from time to time. Under the Consulate he had been Ambassador to Lisbon, during which time he amassed considerable sums of money by rather dubious means. Mortally wounded at Essling, and buried in *Les Invalides*. (Author's Collection)

1806: Became a *chevalier* of the *Couronne de Fer*, 25 February. Fought at Saalfeld, Jena and Pultusk, where he was wounded.

1807: Became ill and, in January, relinquished his command of the V Corps of the *Grande Armée*. Awarded the Grand Cross of the Order of St Henry of Saxony. Recovered, he was appointed commander of the reserve corps of the *Grande Armée*, 5 May, and fought at Danzig, Heilsberg and Friedland. Became *Colonel-Général* of the Swiss regiments of the *Grand Armée* and a *chevalier* of the Order of Saint Andrew of Russia, 13 September.

1808: Became Duke of Montebello, 15 June, then departed for Spain in October. Fought at Tudela, but obliged to give up his command following a bad fall from his horse on 2 December. 20 December, took command of the siege of Saragossa, which fell on 21 February the following year.

1809: Recalled to the *Grande Armée*, he fought at Abensberg, Landshut, Eckmühl and Ratisbonne. Commanded the II Corps of the *Grande Armée* at Aspern-Essling, where he was struck in the knees by a cannonball. Died following amputation of his right leg at Ebersdorff on 31 May.

a peer of the realm and Governor of the 5th Military Division at Strasbourg, 4 June. Awarded the Grand Cross of *Saint-Louis*, 23 August.

1815: Became a peer of the Empire, 2 June, but took no part in the Hundred Days campaign.

## LANNES

Jean Lannes, *Duc de Montebello*, 1769–1809.

1804: Commanded the invasion camp of Ambleteuse when he became a Marshal of France.

1805: Awarded the Grand Cross of Portugal and, 2 June, the Grand Eagle of the Legion of Honour. Commanded the V Corps of the *Grande Armée* at Ulm and Austerlitz.

## LEFEBVRE

François-Joseph Lefebvre, *Duc de Dantzig*, 1755–1820.

1804: Became a Marshal of France, 19 May.

1805: Invested with the Grand Eagle of the Legion of Honour, 2 February.

1806: Replaced Mortier as commander of the V Corps of the *Grande Armée*, 11 September. Appointed commander of the infantry of the Imperial Guard, 5 October, and fought at Jena.

1807: Commanded the X Corps of the *Grande Armée* at the siege of Danzig, 23 January to 24 May. Became Duke of Danzig.

1808: Commanded the IV Corps of the *Armée d'Espagne* and fought at Durango, Santander, Gueñes and Espinosa.

1809: Commanded the VII Corps of the *Grande Armée* and fought at Arnhofen and Eckmühl. Appointed commander of the *Armée du Tyrol* from May to October, and took Innsbruck.

1812: Commanded the infantry of the Old Guard during the Russian campaign and fought at Smolensk, Borodino, Krasnoe and the Berezina.

1813: Recalled to Paris, 11 January, and retired.

1814: Resumed active service, commanding the Old Guard, and fought at Champaubert, Montmirail and Montereau, and then retired.

François-Joseph LEFEBVRE, 1755–1820. A mediocre strategist, but a just, humane and objective man who well-merited his appointment as *Colonel-Général* of the Infantry of the Guard. He wears ceremonial full dress uniform.

Jacques-Etienne-Joseph-Alexandre **MACDONALD**, 1765–1840. Under the Consulate, Macdonald was Ambassador to Copenhagen, 1801–03; but, following his performance on the field of Wagram in 1809, he became a marshal. He was a capable tactician and administrator, and admired for his integrity and loyalty despite having been among the group of marshals who pressed the abdication on the Emperor and then negotiated his exile with the Allies. (Engr. Delorme. Author's Collection)

## MACDONALD

Jacques-Etienne-Joseph-Alexandre Macdonald, *Duc de Tarente*, 1765–1840.

1807: Disgraced since 1804, recalled 28 February to serve the *Armée de Naples*.

1809: Commanded a corps under Prince Eugene and wounded at Piave, 8 May. Fought at Wagram, whereafter he was forgiven his actions of 1804 and, 12 July, awarded the rank of Marshal of France. Invested with the Grand Eagle of the Legion of Honour, 14 August, and became Duke of Tarentum, 9 December.

1810–11: Served in Catalonia from 24 April 1810 to 20 September 1811.

1812: Commanded the X Corps of the *Grande Armée* in Russia and conducted the siege of Riga, August to December.

**Auguste-Frédéric-Louis Viesse de MARMONT, 1744–1852.**
Governor of the Illyrian Provinces, Marmont was a vain,
grasping individual whose pride and greed could not tolerate
Napoleon's paternal and patronizing rule. He went over to the
Bourbons in 1814, accompanying Louis XVIII to Ghent during
the Hundred Days. He remained true to the Bourbons and later
followed Charles X into exile after the Revolution of 1830.
(Engr. Johnson. Author's Collection)

1813: Appointed commander of the XI Corps of
the *Grande Armée*, 10 April, and fought at
Merseburg, Lützen, Bischofswerda,
Bautzen, Katzbach, Leipzig and
Hanau. Led the defence of the Lower
Rhine from November.

1814: Obliged to retreat from Cologne as of
January, he fought at Mormant, Ferté-
sur-Aube, Nogent-sur-Seine, Provins
and Saint-Dizier. Became a peer of

France under the First Restoration, 4
June, and then Governor of the 21st
Military Division at Bourges, 21 June.

1815: Escorted the fleeing Louis XVIII to the
frontier at the beginning of the Hundred
Days, but took no part in the campaign.
With the Second Restoration, he was
appointed commander of the *Armée du
Loire*, which he disbanded.

## MARMONT

Auguste-Frédéric-Louis Viesse de Marmont, *Duc
de Raguse*, 1774–1852.

1805: Appointed *Colonel-Général* of Hussars and
*Chasseurs*, 1 February, and, 2 February,
awarded the Grand Eagle of the Legion
of Honour. Appointed commander of
the II Corps of the *Grande Armée*, 30
August, and fought at Ulm and Weyer.
Assumed command of the I Corps of the
*Armée d'Italie*, 23 December.

1806: Became Governor-General of Dalmatia, 7
July, and raised the siege of Ragusa.

1808: Became Duke of Ragusa, 15 April.

1809: Commanded the XI Corps of the *Grande
Armée* and fought at Gradschatz, Gos-
pich, Fiume, Graz, Wagram and
Znaïm. Became a Marshal of France, 12
July, and Governor of the Illyrian
Provinces in October.

1811: Appointed commander of the VI Corps of
the *Armée de Portugal* in place of Marshal
Ney, 9 April, and eventually became
Commander-in-Chief of the entire army
in place of Masséna, 7 May.

1812: Fought at Salamanca, where he was
gravely wounded. Compelled to surrender his post as a consequence.

1813: Commanded the VI Corps of the *Grande
Armée* at Lützen, Bautzen, Leipzig and
Hanau.

1814: Fought at Brienne, La Rothière, Cham-
paubert, Vauchamps, Montmirail,
Meaux, Gué à Tresmes, Lizy, Reims,
Laon, Fismes, La Fére-Champenoise,
La Ferté-Gaucher and Paris. Sur-

rendered his corps to the allies, 5 April. Became a peer of France, 4 June, under the First Restoration.

1815: Commanded the Household Corps of Louis XVIII in exile at Ghent, following the return of the Emperor. Struck from the roll of Marshals, 10 April. After the Hundred Days, returned with the King and, 3 August, appointed a *major-général* of the *Garde Royale*.

## MASSENA

Andre Masséna, *Duc de Rivoli, Prince d'Essling*, 1758–1817.

1804: Became a Marshal of the Empire, 19 May.

1805: Awarded the Grand Eagle of the Legion of Honour, 2 February. Commanded the *Armée d'Italie* at Caldiero, 30 October. On 11 December, he was given command of the VIII Corps of the *Grande Armée*, but on the 28th was reappointed as Commander-in-Chief of the Army of Naples.

1806: Took up his command at Bologna, 9 January, then invaded the Kingdom of Naples, seizing Capua, 12 February, and entering Naples on the 14th. Directed the I Corps of the Army of Naples in the siege of Gaëta, 26 February to 19 July. Led the Calabrian expedition as from August.

1807: Rejoined the *Grande Armée*, 12 January, and replaced Lannes as commander of the V Corps on 24 February. Retired to Rueil for a well-earned rest, 15 July.

1808: Became Duke of Rivoli, 19 March.

1809: Commanded the IV Corps of the *Grande Armée* at Landshut, Eckmühl, Ebersberg, Aspern-Essling and Wagram.

1810: Became Prince of Essling, 31 January, and awarded the Château de Thouars (Deux-Sèvres). Appointed commander of the *Armée de Portugal*, leaving Paris on 29 April and assuming his command at Valladolid on 10 May. Led his army at Ciudad Rodrigo, Almeida and Busaco before finally halting at the impregnable

André MASSENA, 1758–1817. As a general, Masséna was wily, bold and tenacious, which served him well in the Peninsula and Austrian campaigns. He was also a lecher (going so far as to take his mistress, Mme Leberton, with him to Spain disguised as a soldier), a bare-faced plunderer, and a shameless miser. The illustration show him in full dress riding uniform, 1805–07. (Author's Collection)

lines of Torres Vedras.

1811: Withdrew his army towards Spain as from 6 March and fought at Fuentes d'Onoro, 3 to 5 May. Recalled in disgrace, 7 May, and replaced by Marmont. Appointed commander of the 8th Military Division at Toulon.

1815: Became a peer of the Empire, 2 June, and commanded the Paris National Guard, 22 June to 8 July.

## MONCEY

Bon-Adrien-Jeannot de Moncey, *Duc de Conegliano*, 1754–1842.

1804: Became Marshal of the Empire, 19 May.

1805: Invested with the Grand Eagle of the Legion of Honour.

1807: Appointed commander of the Corps of Observation of the Coasts of the Ocean, 16 December.

1808: Led his corps to Spain, 9 January, and engaged successfully at Los Capreras and unsuccessfully at Valencia. Became Duke of Conegliano, 2 July, and fought at Almanza and Lerin, commanding the III Corps of the *Armée d'Espagne*; and Tudela, following which he directed the siege of Saragossa for a time.

1809–14: Engaged in no military campaigns, but held senior executive posts in Belgium and France.

1814: Appointed *Major-Général* of the National Guard of Paris, 8 January, which he personally led in the defence of the city, notably in the fierce action at the *Barrière de Clichy*, 30 March. Became inspector-general of the *gendarmerie* under the First Restoration and a peer of the realm, 4 June.

1815: Made a peer of the Empire, 2 June. Following the Hundred Days campaign, he declined to preside over Marshal Ney's court martial and was deprived of his rank and title and imprisoned for three months in the fortress of Ham, 29 August.

## MORTIER

Edouard-Adolphe-Casmir-Joseph Mortier, *Duc de Trévise*, 1768–1835.

1804: Became *Colonel-Général* of the Artillery and Marines of the Imperial Guard. Promoted to Marshal of France, 19 May, and made *Commandant* of the 2nd Cohort of the Legion of Honour, 14 June.

1805: Awarded the Grand Eagle of the Legion of Honour, 2 February, and made a *chevalier* of the Order of Christ of Portugal. Appointed *Colonel-Général* of the infantry

Bon-Adrien-Jeannot de MONCEY, 1754–1842. Moncey enlisted as a volunteer in the *Champagne-Infanterie* at the age of fifteen and served almost continuously thereafter, rising steadily through the ranks and achieving the post of *inspecteur-général* of the *gendarmerie* by 3 December 1801. He was the epitomy of an honest, decent and upright commander, holding many important posts under the Empire, but particularly distinguishing himself while personally directing the defence of the *Barrière de Clichy* during the siege of Paris in 1814. He went on to serve the Bourbons, taking the field once more in 1823, when he led the conquest of Catalonia during the Spanish campaign, and becoming Governor of *Les Invalides* in 1833. (Author's Collection)

of the Imperial Guard, 30 August. Commanded a provisional corps of the *Grande Armée*, 7 November to 16 December, and fought at Dürrenstein.

1807: Commanded the VIII Corps of the *Grande Armée* and conquered Hesse and Hanover, occupied Hamburg and Bremen, fought at Anklam and Friedland and laid siege to Colberg.

1808: Became Duke of Treviso, 2 July, and given command of the V Corps of the *Armée d'Espagne*, 2 October. Fought at Somosierra, 30 November.

1809: Covered Lannes' siege of Saragossa, then fought at Arzobispo with Soult, 8 August, and Ocaña, where he was wounded.

1810: Took part in the invasion of Andalusia. Fought at Badajoz and Fuentes de Cantos.

1811: Fought at Gebora and Campo Maior. Recalled to France in May, where he commanded the Young Guard.

1812: Fought at Borodino and made Governor of Moscow. Commanded the rearguard of the *Grande Armée* in the first days of the retreat and fought at Krasnoe and the Berezina.

1813: Fought at Lützen, Bautzen, Dresden and Leipzig. Became commander of the Old Guard in December.

1814: Fought in the campaign of France at Langres, Bar, Montmirail, Château-Thierry, Lizy, Neuilly-St-Front, Craonne, Laon, La Fére-Champenoise and Ferté-Gaucher, and defended Paris with Marmont. Became a *Chevalier de Saint-Louis*, 1 June, a peer of France, 4 June, and then Governor of the 14th Military Division at Lille, 21 June, under the restored Bourbons.

1815: Escorted the fleeing monarch to the frontier upon the return of the Emperor, reverted to Napoleon and given command of the Old Guard. Fell ill at Beaumont and did not take part in the Waterloo campaign. Struck from the roll of peers of the realm by the returned Bourbons, 24 July, then relieved of his command of the 16th Military Division, 27 December. He was, however, reinstated early in the following year.

**Edouard-Adolphe-Casmir-Joseph MORTIER, 1768–1835.** An unusual marshal, in that he managed to combine both courage and a cool head in his exercise of command. A calm and methodical leader, he was also greatly loved in a personal sense by his fellow marshals for his friendly disposition, and was grievously mourned after his death in 1835 in the course of an attempted assassination of King Louis-Philippe. The illustration depicts him in full dress riding uniform. (Engr. Heinemann. Author's Collection)

## MURAT

Joachim, Prince Murat, *Grand-Duc de Berg et de Clèves*, King of Naples, 1767–1815.

1804: Became Governor of Paris, 15 January, then promoted to Marshal of the Empire.

1805: Became Grand Admiral and Prince, 1 February, and awarded the Grand Eagle of the Legion of Honour on the 2nd. Commander-in-Chief of the Cavalry of the *Grande Armée* during the Austerlitz campaign, captured Vienna and fought at Wertigen, Ulm, Amstetten, Dürrenstein and Austerlitz.

1806: Became a Grand Dignitary of the Order of the *Couronne de Fer*, 20 February, and Grand Duke of Cleves-Berg on 15 March. Fought at Jena, Erfürt, Prentzlow and entered Warsaw on 28 November.

1807: Engaged at Hoff, Eylau, Heilsberg and Königsberg.

1808: Appointed Lieutenant of the Empire in Spain, 20 February, and entered Madrid, 24 March. Suppressed the '*Dos de Mayo*' insurrection, but retired from the Peninsula on 15 June on the grounds of poor health. Proclaimed King of Naples, 1 August, and successfully besieged Capri.

1809: Defeated in an expedition against Sicily.

1812: Commanded the Reserve Cavalry of the *Grande Armée* during the Russian campaign and fought at Krasnoe, Ostrowno, Smolensk, Taroutina, Borodino and Winkowo. 5 December, suddenly appointed Commander-in-Chief of the entire *Grande Armée*.

1813: 18 January, promptly delegated his last appointment and deserted the army for Naples. Rejoined the *Grande Armée* in Saxony in August and fought at Dresden, Wachau and Leipzig. 5 November, again departed for the sanctuary of Naples on the pretext of raising fresh troops.

1814: Concluded treaties with Austria and Great Britain which guaranteed his crown in return for a 30,000-strong contingent to fight against France. Seized Reggio and forced Prince Eugene to cede the Adige River frontier.

1815: Swore allegiance to Napoleon following poor relations with the newly deposed Bourbons, and seized Florence. Defeated at Tolentino, 2 May, and fled to France. The Emperor, however, was deaf to his importuning and he found himself in Lyons when the news of Waterloo broke. With a royal reward now offered for his head, he fled first to Toulon, then to Corsica, from where he attempted a return-from-Elba-style *coup* to regain his kingdom. Landed at Pizzo in Calabria with a band of thirty followers and following a brief fracas he was arrested and imprisoned. 13 October, he was tried, found guilty and executed.

Joachim **MURAT**, **1767–1815**. **Although a Marshal of France, Grand Duke and King, Murat is chiefly renowned for his fiery leadership and courage as a cavalry commander, and for his ostentatious taste in dress. Certainly, he was a better cavalryman than head of state, and his undoubted bravery was but poor recommendation to a throne. He owed his appointments purely to his status as brother-in-law to the Emperor through his marriage to Caroline Bonaparte. Napoleon once wrote to him: 'You are a good soldier on the field of battle, but beyond that, you have neither vigour nor character.' His attempts to maintain the throne of Naples by turning on his benefactor in the later years availed him nothing, and he was executed by firing squad after trying to ape his Emperor's return from Elba by a *coup* at Pizzo, Calabria, in 1815. (Author's Collection)**

## NEY

Michel Ney, *Duc d'Elchingen, Prince de la Moskowa*, 1769–1815.

1804: Commanded the invasion camp of Montreuil. Promoted to Marshal of France.

1805: Awarded the Grand Eagle of the Legion of Honour. Commanded the VI Corps of the *Grande Armée* and fought at Elchingen, 14 October. Invaded the Tyrol and seized Innsbruck, 7 November.

1806: Commanded the VI Corps and fought at Jena, captured Erfürt and compelled the capitulation of Magdeburg.

1807: Fought at Eylau, Guttstadt and Friedland.

1808: Became the Duke of Elchingen, 6 June. Appointed commander of the VI Corps of the *Armée d'Espagne*, 2 August, and captured Bilbao, 26 September.

1809: Fought at Baños, 12 August.

1810: Commanded the VI Corps of Masséna's *Armée de Portugal*, 17 April, besieged and took Ciudad Rodrigo, 6 June to 10 July, and Almeida, 24 July to 28 August. Fought at Busaco, then commanded the rearguard of Masséna's army as it retreated from Portugal.

1811: Relieved from his command for insubordination, 23 March. Commanded the *Camp de Boulogne* from 31 August.

1812: Relieved of his command at Boulogne, 1 February. Appointed commander of the III Corps of the *Grande Armée*, 1 April, and fought at Krasnoe, Smolensk and Borodino. Appointed commander of the rearguard of the retreating *Grande Armée*, 3 November, in place of Davout, and fought at the Berezina, 28 November.

1813: Became Prince of the Moskowa, 25 March. Fought at Weissenfels, Lützen, Bautzen, Dresden, Dennewitz and Leipzig. Wounded 18 October and ordered back to France on the 23rd.

1814: Fought in the campaign of France at Brienne, La Rothière, Champaubert, Montmirail, Château-Thierry, Vauchamps, Craonne, Laon, Reims, Châlons-sur-Marne and Arcis-sur-Aube. Following the Emperor's abdication, went over to the Bourbons, becoming Governor of the 6th Military Division at Besançon, 21 May, a *Chevalier de Saint-Louis*, 1 June, and a peer of France, 4 June. Appointed Commander-in-Chief of the *Corps Royale de Cavalerie*.

1815: Dispatched to arrest the returned Emperor, went over to his side, 12 March, becoming a peer of the Empire, 2 June. Summoned to the *Armée du Nord*, 11

Michel NEY, 1769–1815. The most renowned of Napoleon's marshals, Michel Ney was a soldier of exceptional ability, particularly in the most difficult of circumstances, and aptly dubbed 'the bravest of the brave' and 'the indefatigable'. Best known for his courage, Ney was nonetheless a skilful commander with a thorough knowledge of his profession. He was condemned to death for his part in the Hundred Days campaign and shot dead by firing squad in Paris, under the Second Restoration. (Gérard. Engr. Tietze. Author's Collection)

June, and fought at Fleurus, Quatre-Bras and Waterloo. Following the defeat, retired to the Château de la Bessonie (Cantal), where he was arrested, 3 August. Tried 4 December and found guilty of treason on the 6th. Shot on 7 December.

## OUDINOT

Nicolas-Charles Oudinot, *Duc de Reggio*, 1769–1851.

1805: Replaced Junot as commander of the Reserve of Grenadiers at Arras, 5 February. Invested with the Grand Eagle of the Legion of Honour, 6 March. Wounded at Hollabrünn, 16 November, and obliged to resign his command.

1806: Commanded the 2nd Foot Dragoons attached to the Imperial Guard.

1807: Fought at Ostrolenka, then took part in the siege of Danzig, of which he assumed command, 24 May, in place of Lefebvre. Fought at Friedland.

1808: Became a Count of the Empire, 2 July.

1809: Fought with the II Corps at Essling and Wagram, following which he was promoted to Marshal of France 12 July.

1810: Became Duke of Reggio, 14 April.

1811: Commander of the *II Corps d'Observation*.

1812: Commanded the II Corps of the *Grande Armée* in Russia. Wounded at Polotsk and obliged to relinquish his command, 18 August. Resumed command in October, but wounded at the Berezina, 28 November, and again on the 30th.

1813: Fought with the XII Corps at Bautzen, Leipzig and Grossbeeren.

1814: Fought at Brienne, where he was wounded, La Rothière, Saint-Dizier and Arcis-sur-Aube (commanding the VIII Corps), where he was again wounded. Appointed commander of the *Corps Royale de Grenadiers et Chasseurs de France*, 20 May, under the restored Bourbons. Became a commander of *Saint-Louis*, 2 June, and a peer of France, 4 June. Appointed Governor of the 3rd Military Division at Metz.

1815: Took no part in the Hundred Days campaign.

## PERIGNON

Cathérine-Dominique, *Marquis de Pérignon*, 1754–1818.

1804: Became a Marshal of France, 19 May.

1805: Awarded the Grand Eagle of the Legion of Honour, 2 February.

1806: Appointed Governor-General of the States of Parma and Plasencia, 18 September.

1808: Became Governor of Naples, 23 July, commanding the *Armée de Naples* under King Joachim (Murat). Became Grand Dignitary of the Order of the Two Sicilies, 9 October.

1813: Retired, 27 March.

Nicolas-Charles OUDINOT, 1767–1847. Promoted to the rank of marshal on the field of Wagram, in place of Marshal Lannes, Oudinot was a mediocre strategist but an exceptionally brave and intrepid leader of men. Under the Second Restoration he became a *Major-Général* of the *Garde Royale* and, in 1823, commanded the I Corps in the invasion of Spain. Despite a score of wounds acquired in the course of his campaigns, he went on to become Governor of *Les Invalides* and died at the late age of eighty. (Engr. Forestier. Author's Collection)

1814: Following Napoleon's abdication, he was reinstated and appointed the King's commissioner extraordinary to the 1st Military Division, 31 May to 10 October. Became a *Chevalier de Saint-Louis*, 1 June, and then a peer of France, 4 June.

1815: Although appointed Governor of Toulouse, 28 March, he retired to Montech. With his return, the Emperor struck his name from the roll of Marshals, 10 April, but, 24 July, he was reinstated by the returned Louis XVIII.

## PONIATOWSKI

Prince Josef Anton Poniatowski, 1763–1813.

1807: Became commander of the 1st Polish Legion in French service, 2 January.

1808: Appointed Minister of War of the Grand Duchy of Warsaw with the rank of *Generalissimo*.

burg, Chemnitz, Penig and Leipzig, 16 to 18 October. Became a Marshal of France, 16 October. Cut off from the *Grande Armée*, 19 October, led a last charge and then, despite four wounds, attempted to swim the River Elster, in which he drowned.

## SERURIER
Jean-Mathieu-Philibert, *Comte Sérurier*, 1742–1819.

1804: Became Governor of *Les Invalides*, 23 April, then a Marshal of France, 19 May.
1805: Awarded the Grand Eagle of the Legion of Honour and the Grand Cordon of the *Couronne de Fer*.
1808: Became Count Sérurier.
1809: Appointed commander of the National Guard of Paris, 3 September.
1810: Appointed President of the Court of Inquiry into General Decaen's surrender of the *Ile de France*, 3 December.
1814: Became a peer of France under the First Restoration, 4 June.
1815: Awarded a peerage under the returned Emperor, 2 June. With the Second Restoration, he was retired from his post as Governor of the *Invalides*, 27 December.

## SOULT
Nicolas-Jean de Dieu Soult, *Duc de Dalmatie*, 1769–1851.

1804: Commander of the Saint-Omer invasion camp. 19 May, promoted to Marshal of France and *Colonel-Général* of the Imperial Guard.
1805: Invested with the Grand Eagle of the Legion of Honour, 2 February. Commanded the IV Corps of the *Grande Armée* and fought at Austerlitz.
1806–07: Fought at Jena, Eylau and Heilsberg; received the surrender of Königsberg. Awarded the Swedish Order of the Seraphims, the Bavarian Order of Saint Hubert and the Spanish Order of the Golden Fleece.
1808–09: Became Duke of Dalmatia, 29 June

**Cathérine-Dominique, *Marquis de* PERIGNON, 1754–1818.** Pérignon was one of the four honorary marshals created in 1804 and, though he held important administrative posts during the Empire, his active service took place during the Revolutionary Wars. (Hennequin. Author's Collection)

1809: Awarded the Grand Eagle of the Legion of Honour and the Grand Cordon of the Military Order of the Grand Duchy of Warsaw. Fought at Fallenti, 19 April, and occupied Cracow in July.
1812: Commanded the V Corps (Polish) of the *Grande Armée*, 3 March, and fought at Smolensk and Borodino. Wounded at the Berezina, 26 November.
1813: Commanded the VIII Corps (Polish) of the *Grande Armée*, 12 March, invaded Bohemia and fought at Lobau, Alten-

**Prince Josef Anton PONIATOWSKI, 1763–1813.** Nephew of King Stanislas-Augustus, Prince Poniatowski was a chivalrous and courageous man who excelled in the field. Promoted to marshal on the first day of the battle of Leipzig, he tragically drowned three days later in an attempt to swim the River Elster to rejoin the *Grande Armée*, from which he had been cut off. He was dubbed the '*Bayard polonais*', and greatly admired by the Emperor and Davout. (Engr. State. Author's Collection)

1808. Campaigned with the II Corps in the Peninsula: fought at Corunna; invaded Portugal; and engaged at El Arzobispo. Became Chief of Staff to King Joseph in place of Jourdan, 16 September, and fought at Ocaña.

1810: Invaded Andalusia in January and took Seville in February.

1811: Laid siege to Olivença, 11 to 22 January, then Badajoz, which fell 11 March. Declining to reinforce Masséna before Torres Vedras, he then retired to Andalusia. Defeated at Albuera, 16 May, while attempting to raise the British siege of Badajoz. Invaded Grenada and fought at Venta del Bahul, 9 August.

1812: Set out once again to relieve Badajoz only to find that it had fallen to Wellington on 6 April. Having united his army with that of Suchet in Valencia, 1 September, he took the offensive, re-entered Madrid, 2 November, then pursued Wellington's force in its retreat upon Ciudad Rodrigo.

1813: Recalled to France, 3 January, and appointed commander of the Old Guard, 30 April, then commander of the entire Imperial Guard in place of Bessières, 2 May. Fought at Bautzen, then made Commander-in-Chief of the *Armées d'Espagne et des Pyrénées*, July 6. Assumed command at Bayonne, 12 July, then undertook the battles of the Pyrenees, 25 July to 1 August.

1814: Fought at Orthez and Toulouse. With the return of the monarchy, he was relieved of his command, 22 April, then appointed commander of the 13th Military Division at Rennes, 21 June. Became a *Chevalier de Saint-Louis*, 24 September, then promoted to Minister of War, 3 December.

1815: With Napoleon's return he rallied to the Emperor, becoming a peer of France, 2 June, then Chief of Staff to the *Armée du Nord*. Following Waterloo, he rallied the *Grande Armée* at Laon, where he delegated command to Grouchy, 26 June, and retired to Saint-Amans. Struck from the roll of Marshals on 27 December and then exiled, 12 January 1816.

## SUCHET
Louis-Gabriel Suchet, *Duc d'Albufera*, 1770–1826.

1805: Divisional Commander of the *Grande Armée*. Fought at Ulm, Hollabrünn, Austerlitz.

1806: Invested with the Grand Eagle of the Legion of Honour, 8 February. Fought at Saalfeld, Jena and Pultusk.

1807: Fought at Ostrolenka, then given the 1st Division of the V Corps of the *Grande Armée*, 24 February, to which he was given provisional command in August.

1808: Became a *chevalier* of the *Couronne de Fer*, commander of the Order of Saint Henry of Saxony and, 19 March, Count of the Empire. Appointed divisional commander in the *Armée d'Espagne*.

1809: Appointed commander of the III Corps and then Commander-in-Chief of the *Armée d'Aragon*; fought at Saragossa, Maria and Belchite.

1810: Fought at Valencia, Lerida, Mequinenza and Tortosa; laid siege to Tarragona.

1811: The fall of Tarragona, 28 June, led to his becoming a Marshal of France, 8 July. Fought at La Puebla de Benequasil and Sagunto, where he was wounded; laid siege to Valencia.

1812: Following the fall of Valencia, 10 January, became Duke of Albufera, 24 January.

1813: Fought at Castalla and raised the siege of Tarragona. Became Governor of Catalonia, 15 November, then replaced Bessières as *Colonel-Général* of the Imperial Guard, 18 November.

1814: Fought at Molins del Rey and appointed Commander-in-Chief of the Army of the South, 22 April. With the First Restoration he became a peer of France, 4 June, and a commander of *Saint-Louis*, 24 September.

1815: With the return of the Emperor, he was appointed Commander-in-Chief of the *Armée des Alpes*, 26 April, and invaded Savoy, 14 to 30 June. Concluded an armistice with the invading Austrian Army, 12 July. With the Second Restoration he was deprived of command and struck from the list of peers of France.

## VICTOR

Claude Victor-Perrin, *dit* Victor, *Duc de Bellune*, 1764–1841.

1805: Appointed Minister Plenipotentiary to Denmark, 19 February, and, 6 March, awarded the Grand Eagle of the Legion of Honour.

1806: Appointed Chief of Staff to Marshal Lannes, 7 October, fought at Saalfeld and Jena, and signed the capitulation of Spandau, 25 October.

**Jean-Mathieu-Philibert, *Comte* SERURIER, 1742–1819.** A veteran of the Seven Years War, Sérurier was somewhat out of place under both the Revolutionary and Empire régimes. He was another of the honorary marshals of 1804, and was Governor of *Les Invalides* for the duration of the Empire. He is illustrated in undress riding uniform. (Laneuville. Author's Collection)

1807: Fought at Pultusk, then given command of Dombrovski's Polish Division, 4 January, and then the X Corps of the *Grande Armée*, 5 January. Captured by Prussians, 20 January, but exchanged on 8 March. Took charge of the siege of Graudenz, 23 May, then replaced Bernadotte as commander of the I Corps of the *Grande Armée*, 6 June, and fought at Friedland. Awarded a Marshal's baton, 13 July, and appointed Governor of Prussia and of Berlin, 9 August.

1808: Became Duke of Bellune, 10 September. Commanded the I Corps of the *Armée d'Espagne* from 7 September, and fought

**Nicolas-Jean de Dieu SOULT, 1769–1851.** Soult was a prudent and sensible commander with a gift for organization and strategy which shone during the battles for the Pyrenees in 1814. According to Napoleon he was one of the foremost strategists of Europe, which is debatable, but he was certainly one of the ablest of the marshals. He ran Masséna a close second in love of money, and amassed a fortune through handsome annuities from satellite states and plunder. It has been said that Soult lacked initiative; doubtless this would have endeared him to the Emperor, but he was certainly not short on ambition, and managed to become Minister of War to Louis XVIII during the First Restoration, and later Minister of War and Foreign Affairs to Louis-Philippe. He was the last of the Marshals of 1804, dying aged eighty-two, having held his baton for forty-three years, for four years of which he had been one of only four *Maréchaux-Généraux* in French history—an honour bestowed upon him in 1847. (Author's Collection)

at Espinosa, Cadiz, Somosierra and the capture of Madrid.

1809: Fought at Uclés, Medellin, Alcabon and Talavera.

1810–11: Took part in the invasion of Andalusia and fought at Chiclana.

1812: Surrendered his command, 9 February, returned to France and appointed commander of the IX (Reserve) Corps of the *Grande Armée*, 3 April. Fought at the Berezina.

1813: Fought with the II Corps at Dresden and Leipzig.

1814: Fought at Saint-Dizier, Brienne, La Rothière, Montereau and Craonne, where he was wounded. Became Governor of the 2nd Military Division at Mézières, under the First Restoration.

1815: Attempted to organize resistance to the returned Emperor at Châlons-sur-Marne, 16 March, then fled to Ghent to join the King in exile. Struck from the list of Marshals, 10 April. Returned with Louis XVIII, 8 July, made a peer of the realm, 17 August, and a *major-général* of the Royal Guard, 8 September.

# Uniforms and Accessories

Due to lack of space, we are confined to sketching only the broad outlines of the subject of marshals' dress; but the reader will find that many of the finer points of detail are discussed in the captions.

## Headgear

Marshals wore one of two forms of *chapeau*. The first was that employed in ceremonial dress: it consisted of a black felt cap and brim, the latter turned up at the front only, of the pattern devised for Princes of the Empire, ornamented with a loop of gold lace and a brace of white ostrich plumes. The second variety was utilized in all but court dress, and consisted of a *général de division*'s bicorn with gold lace about the exterior perimeter of the brim, gold pulls in the angles, a gold loop about a *tricolor* cockade, and a *panache* of white ostrich plumes and white *aigrette* on top. The silhouette of this latter headgear altered almost imperceptibly over the years, becoming taller and narrower, the *panache* of ostrich plumes eventually being replaced by a feather-stitch of white plumes about the interior perimeter of the brim, and the gold lace of the exterior perimeter often being neglected altogether.

**Murat (1) with his aide Captain Manhés (2) Eylau, February 1807.**

A

Soult (1) with a captain ADC (2) and Adjudant-Commandant (3) at Corunna, January 1809.

B

CHRIS WARNER

**Masséna (2) with a captain of Ingénieurs géographes (1) and his son and ADC, Count Prosper d'Essling (3) before the Lines of Torres Vedras, autumn 1810.**

**Lannes (2) with his escort commander, an officer of the 1st Light Horse Lancers of the Vistula Legion (1) and a lieutenant of the 1st Infantry of the Vistula Legion (3) before Saragossa, 1809.**

Suchet (2) with a trumpeter of the 13th Cuirassiers (1) and his ADC (3) at Sagunto, 25 October 1811.

CHRIS WARNER

E

**Davout with his Emperor:
Borodino, 6 September 1812.**

F

**Berthier (1) with an ADC (2) and Adjudant-Commandant (3), 1812-13.**

G

Ney (2) with a Fusilier of the 95th Line Infantry (1) and a trooper of the 1st Cuirassiers (3) at Waterloo, 18 June 1815.

H

## Tunics:

*Ceremonial dress*

'The uniform of Marshals of the Empire will be deep blue, in silk, velvet or linen, and embroidered along all seams with the same design employed by staff officers, but one third larger.' (Extract from the *Décret du 29 messidor, an XII* [18 July 1804]. This heavily embellished *habit* was worn for all formal and state occasions. It had no turnbacks to the skirt and was worn without epaulettes.

*Full dress*

'The blue habit will be as prescribed by the regulation of 1er vendémiaire, an XII, for the undress uniform of généraux de division, except that the embroidery shall be larger by a third. There will also be two marshals' batons on each epaulette in place of stars. . . . The buttons will be embossed with a garland of leaves, half oak and half laurel, [and] with two crossed marshals' batons tied together with the ribbon of the Legion of Honour.' (Extract from the *Décret du 26 fructidor, an XII* [13 September 1804].) The full dress tunic was basically a replica of that employed in ceremonial dress, save that it was worn with epaulettes and generally manufactured from hard-wearing linen in place of silk or velvet.

*Undress*

This *habit* was a still cheaper replica of the ceremonial dress tunic, with no pockets, or lace to simulate them, on the skirt; no embroidery on the sleeve or back seams; but with turnbacks on the skirt, embellished with marshals' lace and the insignia common to all staff officers.

*Campaign dress*

On campaign, marshals wore a comparatively plain *habit*, resembling a *surtout*, with lace on the collar and cuffs only. The skirt was stitched with false turnbacks, devoid of ornament save for the gold staff officers' device.

## Epaulettes

The epaulettes were those of a *général de division* with batons, embroidered in blue silk, in place of stars, though some marshals (e.g. Davout's undress tunic, preserved in the *Musée de l'Armée*) persisted in retaining stars on theirs, up to the number of five (e.g. Bernadotte). By reason of office, some marshals wore aiguillettes in addition to their epaulettes in full dress:

Claude Victor-Perrin, VICTOR, 1764–1841. Victor only became a marshal in 1807, and was a nonchalant, though courageous, fellow whose personality clashed sharply with Napoleon's. As a consequence of their sour relationship he readily rallied to the Bourbons at the First Restoration, following Louis XVIII into exile in 1815. Under the Second Restoration he was rewarded with the rank of *Major-Général* of the *Garde Royale* and became a peer of France. He later fell into disfavour and disgrace after the Revolution of 1830. (Lith. Delpech. Author's Collection)

Berthier, as *Major-Général* of the *Grande Armée*, 1807–14.

Lefebvre, as intermittent Commander-in-Chief of the infantry of the Guard.

Those marshals appointed *colonels-généraux* of the Guard:

Davout of the *Grenadiers à Pied*.

Soult of the *Chasseurs à Pied*.

Bessières of the cavalry.

Mortier of the artillery and marines.

## Sash

The marshals' sashes varied from individual to individual, and the regulation gold ground-cloth pattern was replaceable with white silk varieties ornamented with three lateral bands of gold, or speckled with gold points, or friezes of stars

embroidered in gold thread. The tassels were not necessarily embellished with blue silk batons; many were decorated with either stars or Imperial eagles instead.

## Baton

'They will carry a baton 5 décimétres (50cm) in length, in blue, sewn with gold eagles of 4cm in diameter.' (Extract from the *Décret du 29 messidor, an XII* [18 July 1804].) The marshals carried their batons from March 1805. They were covered in blue velvet and ornamented with four rows of eight Imperial eagles. The ferrules at each end were gold and engraved '*Terror belli. Decus pacis*' at the top; and the first and second name of the marshal followed by '. . . *nommé par l'Empereur Napoléon, maréchal de l'Empire, le 29 Floréal An XII* [19 May 1804]' at the bottom.

## Saddles and Harness

In principle, the crimson *schabraques* of the marshals were identical to those employed by the *généraux de division*, with the addition of a gold coil fringe 7cm deep about the exterior perimeter. This regulation was certainly never universally adhered to, and variations abound: the crimson velvet saddle proper was frequently embellished with the interwoven oak and laurel-leaf motif embroidered in gold about the cantle and side-panels; the pistol holsters, covers and *schabraque* proper might bear the regulation flat gold laces (one 6cm and the other 2·5cm in depth), but which lace edged the exterior was a personal choice (despite such recommendations as the 1812 regulations, which specified that the slimmer lace was to edge the exterior perimeter). Alternatively, the *schabraque* and holster covers might bear embroidery of the same pattern as that described on the saddle proper. All leathers employed in the harness and bridle were black. All metal parts, including stirrups, were gold and heavily worked with decorative motifs.

**Louis-Gabriel SUCHET, 1770–1826. A brilliant and rare combination of exceptional administrator and field commander, Suchet became a marshal in 1811, following his successes in Spain. He was virtually the only marshal to return from the Peninsula with any credit to his name. Rallied to Napoleon in the Hundred Days, he was strangely only accorded a small secondary rôle, for which he was duly ostracized from society under the Second Restoration. He wears full dress riding uniform. (Engr. Muller. Author's Collection)**

**Full dress uniform, foot duty. The *grand uniforme à pied* consisted of the ceremonial dress tunic, waistcoat, breeches, silk stockings and shoes. The headgear employed in both this and full ceremonial dress was a black general's bicorn, embellished with gold lace and decorated with *tricolor* cockade, gold loop and pulls, and a *panache* of white ostrich plumes with a white *aigrette*. (Bucquoy. Courtesy De Gerlache de Gomery Collection)**

Ceremonial full dress. Drawn from contemporary portraits, this illustration shows Marshals Moncey and Lefebvre in regulation ceremonial dress conforming to the decree of *29 messidor, an XII* (18 July 1804). The *habit* could be of silk, velvet or linen cloth, and was embroidered about all exterior edges and seams with a garland of interwoven oak and laurel leaves, representing Strength and Glory. Beneath this was worn a white waistcoat, embroidered in like fashion. The velvet cape is indigo blue, lined in white silk and ornamented in similar manner, but with a replica of the insignia of the Grand Eagle of the Legion of Honour in addition. (Bucquoy. Courtesy De Gerlache de Gomery Collection)

# *The Plates*

*Plate A: Prince Murat at Eylau, 8 February 1807*

Having bungled badly and repeatedly, and been publicly rebuked for his conduct in the Austerlitz campaign, we here see Murat at the zenith of his extremely erratic military career. From being Napoleon's 'harlequin brother-in-law', he had, through his actions in the Prussian campaign of the previous year, re-established at least the possibility that he was a conscientious and efficient commander of the Reserve Cavalry. Now he was about

to silence doubts as to his ability, leading a charge of eighty squadrons, 10,000 men, straight into the heart of the bloody battle. Visible in the background are the silhouettes of d'Hautpoul's *cuirassiers*, the only cavalry to breach the squares of the redoubtable Russian infantry on that day.

*A1* shows Prince Murat, Grand Duke of Berg and Cleves, in full dress. Murat is dressed in one of his less extravagant uniforms, basically a white marshal's uniform with the Hungarian breeches and boots common to light cavalry marshals. It was seemingly only after he became King of Naples, in 1808, that his costumes became proportionally more bizarre as his credibility decreased. He has removed the aiguillettes from his right shoulder in order to keep his sword-arm free.

*A2* is *Capitaine* Manhés, *aide-de-camp* to Marshal Murat, in campaign dress. The marshals averaged about a half-dozen ADCs apiece on campaign. Here we have illustrated *Capitaine* Manhés, known to be in Murat's service at this period (along with the celebrated diarist Marbot). The dolman beneath the captain's pelisse was crimson with buff collar and cuffs, and gold lace and braid. An alternative to the colpack headgear shown here was the early pattern of the 1806 model shako, in crimson with gold upper band, gold *raquettes* and cords, and yellow plume and pompon.

*Plate B: Marshal Soult at Corunna, 16–18 January 1809*

If not his first, then certainly his greatest early encounter with the British: Marshal Soult had cautiously stalked their army, under Sir John Moore, KB, some 400km in the previous two weeks. Arrived at Corunna, the Marshal was his usual prudent self and wasted several days sensibly reconnoitring the port, while the British sweated out the arrival of their fleet and salvation. Soult finally launched his siege and bombardment of the city but, impressed by the resistance met by the first of his divisions to engage, he called off the action and calmly watched the evacuation of the 'BEF' from Spanish soil. It would seem he was temporizing: why risk a battle—and he greatly admired Moore's handling of the retreat—when the same ends could be achieved without bloodshed?

*B1* illustrates Marshal Soult, *Major-Général* of the *Armée d'Espagne*, in *petite tenue* and cape. The undress *habit* was similar, but more simple than the full-dress tunic in that it lacked the heavily embroidered pockets on the skirt and was devoid of lace on the sleeve and back seams. The Marshal's cape is of the same pattern as those employed by *généraux de division*, but differed in that the embroidery of oak and laurel leaves about the collar and short shoulder-cape was larger by one-third.

*B2* shows a *Capitaine aide-de-camp* to Marshal Soult in undress uniform, 1808–09. The dress of ADCs was as anarchic as that of musicians, and they often designed their own, in addition to wearing the latest fantasies of their superiors. This officer was probably seconded from a light cavalry regiment (2nd Hussars?) and wears the *habit de petite tenue* in place of the more conventional dolman and pelisse. Note the armband on his left arm: these *brassards* were emblems of the wearers' status of ADC and were miniature replicas of their respective superior's waist sash. Thus, the ADC to a marshal wore a white and gold brassard, while the ADCs to a *général de division* and a *général de brigade* wore armbands of red and gold, and sky-blue and gold, respectively.

*B3* is an *Adjutant-Commandant* in full dress, 1809. Originally founded in 1790, the corps of *Adjutants-Généraux* was later renamed *Adjutants-Commandants* by General Bonaparte in July 1800. These senior staff officers were individually assigned to each division of the *Grande Armée* as Chief of Staff, and entrusted to direct and organize the day's rate of march, billets, camp layout, and nourishment of all regiments within the division. Officers of the rank of colonel were frequently appointed assistant chiefs of staff to entire army corps, charged with the onerous task of performing the administrative details behind the movements of thousands of men and horses.

*Plate C: Marshal Masséna before the Lines of Torres Vedras, 1810–11*

Masséna had successfully led the *Armée de Portugal* through such actions as Ciudad Rodrigo and Almeida, and despite Busaco, obliged Wellington's army continually to shorten its supply lines by

**Full dress uniform, mounted duty, 1804 regulations. The *grand uniforme à cheval* was little different from that of foot duty, save that the stockings and shoes were obviously exchanged for French-pattern riding boots. We can see, however, that according to the official edict the *grand cordon* suspending the Legion of Honour medal over the right shoulder was removed to reveal the *baudrier porte-glaive*, a white leather crossbelt and frog into which the marshals' ceremonial sabre was inserted. Note also the use of indigo blue breeches in place of white or buff. (Bucquoy. Courtesy De Gerlache de Gomery Collection)**

retreating. But he was robbed of his expected prize when the British reached the sanctuary of their lines of fortifications, of which he had been entirely ignorant. As tenacious as he was cunning, Masséna carefully reconnoitred the positions for flaws; riding with his staff from vantage point to vantage point with his superb telescope (pilfered from Coimbra University, a typical Masséna touch), probing the fortress for a loophole.

*C1* illustrates a *Capitaine* of the *Ingénieurs-Géographes* in campaign dress, 1810. The *Ingénieurs-Géographes* were created on 30 January 1809 as a new topographical branch of the regular Engineers. The establishment consisted of four *colonels*; four *chefs d'escadron*; twenty-four *capitaines de 1ère Classe*; twenty-four *capitaines de 2eme Classe*; and six *pupilles* of the rank of *sous-lieutenant* and under. The mass of manpower for the ranks was to be drawn from the pupils of the *Ecole Polytechnique*. Their principal concerns were with survey work and the production of maps of entire theatres of operations; as such, they were staff officers basically, forming a pool of

Full dress uniform, mounted duty, actual uniform. In contrast to the previous monochrome plate this illustration depicts the habitual mode of full dress uniform. Note the differences: the *panache* of ostrich feathers has been discarded from the bicorn and replaced by a white feather-stitch lining; the *grand cordon* of the Legion of Honour is still worn, and the ornamental sabre exchanged for a more businesslike personal model; in place of the ceremonial *habit*, a second *habit*, with buttons and loops for the epaulettes, is employed; finally, the familiar white or buff breeches replace the indigo pattern of the 1804 regulations. (Bucquoy. Courtesy De Gerlache de Gomery Collection)

**M²ˡ Victor**
**Duc de Bellune**

**M²ˡ Oudinot**
**Duc de Reggio**

Regulation cape and greatcoat. Both the *manteau trois-quart* and the *redingote* were of similar pattern and colour to those of the *généraux de division*, i.e. plain indigo blue with embroidered garlands of intertwined oak and laurel leaves in gold about the collar and, for the *redingote*, the cuffs. (Bucquoy. Courtesy De Gerlache de Gomery Collection)

manpower from which the various corps or divisions drew their respective chief of staff's requirement for his personal general staff.

*C2* is Marshal Masséna, Commander-in-Chief of the *Armée de Portugal*, in campaign dress, 1810–11. Masséna obstinately prowled outside the fortress for several months, hoping for fresh developments. He questioned his Portuguese staff officers as to their

Marshal Ney in two well-recorded greatcoats. On the left we
see him during the Russian retreat in 1812, after Yvon's
'*Marshal Ney sustaining the rearguard of the Grand Army*'.
On the right we see the Marshal after Meissonier's '*Campaign
of France, 1814*'. (Bucquoy. Courtesy De Gerlache de Gomery
Collection)

Marshal Soult in full dress uniform of *Colonel-Général* of the *Chasseurs à Pied de la Garde*, 1804–14. In their dual capacity as both marshals and *colonels-généraux*, certain marshals had the option of either uniform. As commander of the *Chasseurs*, Soult was one of these and the above illustration is after de Rudder's famous portrait, which now hangs in the Palace of Versailles. The uniform is basically that of an officer of *chasseurs*, with the ornaments of marshals' rank, including the aiguillettes of a *colonel-général* of the Guard. The most unusual feature of the whole is the gold embroidery on his white breeches, which, though conforming to the garland motif of a marshal's lace, is exceptional on an infantry commander. (Van Huen. Courtesy De Gerlache de Gomery Collection)

knowledge of the constructions: they had none, but pointed out that the English must have been very busy indeed to construct such formidable fortifications. 'Without doubt,' he replied, 'but it was not Wellington that made the mountains.' His patience exhausted, his army near-starving, he

raised his siege in March 1811. He wears the marshals' equivalent to the *surtout*, the *frac*: an inexpensive and comfortable campaign tunic. The turnbacks would be identical to those depicted on Marshal Suchet in Plate E.

*C3* is Count Prosper d'Essling, *aide-de-camp* to Marshal Masséna, 1809–10. Prosper was Masséna's son as well as his ADC, a rôle in which he was first recorded the previous year, at the age of sixteen.

*Plate D: Marshal Lannes at the siege of Saragossa, December 1808–February 1809*

One of the first cities to become a centre of resistance to the French overlords after the '*Dos de Mayo*' revolt was Saragossa, ancient capital of Aragon. It endured two bloody sieges before finally falling to Marshals Lannes and Mortier in February. More than a third of the city had been razed, and those structures that still stood all bore the scars of the extended French bombardments. Lannes was horrified at the extent of force he was required to use in quelling the fierce resistance offered by the civilian population of the city, and wrote: 'I have made a count of [Spanish] persons who died in Saragossa from 21 December to 21 February, the day of our entry into the city. . . . 54,000 people have died: it is inconceivable . . . it is impossible that Saragossa should ever recover; this city is a horror to behold.' (Lannes to Berthier, 19 March 1809)

*D1* is an officer of the *1er Chevau-Légers Lanciers* of the *Légion de la Vistule*, 1809. The Vistula Legion was part of Junot's Corps which Lannes, as commander of the left wing of the French Army, employed in his victory at Tudela as well as the second siege of Saragossa. The lancers were the first light cavalry of their type in the *Grande Armée*, and the regiment particularly distinguished itself during the siege. Such was the tenacity of the Spanish defence that the Polish Legion of the Vistula, which took part in every assault on the breaches and resisted each sortie of the defenders, lost more than a third of its effectives before the city was brought to heel.

*D2* shows Marshal Lannes in foot undress uniform, 1808–09. The *petite tenue à pied* consisted of the *habit de petite tenue*, a cheaper and less embellished tunic than those employed in full or ceremonial dress, and regular sash and breeches, but with silk stockings and shoes in place of riding boots. Similarly, the curved sabre affected when mounted would be exchanged for a straight-bladed *épée*, suspended from a frogged waistbelt.

*D3* illustrates a lieutenant of fusiliers of the *1er Régiment d'Infanterie* of the *Légion de la Vistule*, in campaign dress of 1808–09. The Vistula Legion comprised four regiments of infantry in addition to the regiment of lancers. The regiments were structured on the French model and consisted of companies of *grenadiers*, *voltigeurs* and *fusiliers*. The regiments were identified by the colour of their facings:

    1st Regiment: Blue collar, yellow lapels
    2nd Regiment: Yellow collar, yellow lapels
    3rd Regiment: Yellow collar, blue lapels
    4th Regiment: Blue collar, blue lapels

    In the same way as French regiments, where the facing was the ground colour of the uniform, it was piped in the distinctive colour, and vice versa.

*Plate E: Marshal Suchet at Sagunto, 25 October 1811*
Despite Marshal Masséna's attempt to beat the Anglo-Portuguese army decisively prior to the impasse of the lines of Torres Vedras (see Plate C), and his counter-attack which led to defeat at Fuentes d'Onoro, 5 May 1811, it would be wrong to assume that the war in the Peninsula was going badly for France. Portugal might remain inviolate, but in eastern Spain a French general of considerable talent was going from strength to strength: having pacified Catalonia (the battles of Rosas, 1808, and Figueras, 1811) and Aragon (the battles of Lerida, 1810, and Tortosa and Tarragona, 1811), *Général de Division* Suchet was rewarded with a marshal's baton on 5 July 1811. Shortly thereafter, while investing the town of Sagunto, the marshal was caught unawares by the Spanish General Blake, who, with an army 30,000 strong, sought to envelop his single corps. Were it not for the impulsive action of *Capitaine* de Gonneville of the *13eme Cuirassiers* which played a decisive rôle in the French victory, the day might well have been lost and Suchet driven from the field. As it was, however, Suchet's success against Blake at Sagunto led directly to the fall of Valencia later that year.

Marshal Soult, Duke of Dalmatia and *Colonel-Général* of the *Chasseurs à Pied de la Garde*, 1807–14. Here we see Soult in a more everyday full dress. Note that the cuffs of his gloves have been embellished with marshals' lace and, in this instance, we can discern that the seams of his tunic sleeves are also so embroidered, in like manner to his *grand uniforme* marshal's *habit*. (Bucquoy. Courtesy De Gerlache de Gomery Collection)

*E1* is a trumpeter of the *13eme Régiment de Cuirassiers*, 1811. The 13th Cuirassiers shared Suchet's triumphs of Maria, Castellon de la Plana, Lerida, Tortosa, Uldecona and Tarragona, with the *4eme Régiment de Hussards* and the *24eme Régiment de*

**Marshal Davout, Duke of Auerstädt,** *Colonel-Général* **of the** *Grenadiers à Pied de la Garde*, **1804–14. Unlike Soult, Davout wears the basic uniform of a** *grenadier* **with plain gold lace about all facings save collar and cuffs, on which the marshal's lace is utilized. Note also the unusual way in which he wears his sash, beneath the** *habit*. **(Feist. Courtesy De Gerlache de Gomery Collection)**

*Dragons*. At Sagunto, the 4th Hussars and the first squadron of the 13th Cuirassiers were routed when General Caro's 1,500 Spanish cavalry fell upon them; the Spaniard's pursuit of the shattered French cavalry, however, was such a scrimmage that a single squadron of the cuirassiers was sufficient not only to stem their advance but, with General Caro wounded and made prisoner, also to reverse the situation entirely and save the day.

*E2* shows Marshal Suchet in campaign dress, 1811. In the midst of the action Suchet was struck in the right shoulder by a musketball. He is dressed in the *frac* tunic, a plain *surtout*-style *habit*, habitually worn by marshals in the field. Note the turnback devices, common to all staff officers. His wound was far from fatal, and he recovered to blockade and besiege Valencia, which duly fell to him on 10 January 1812.

*E3* is a *capitaine*, *aide-de-camp* to Marshal Suchet, in campaign dress, 1811–12. Sabre drawn, the ADC calls for the surgeon or medical orderlies while standing guard over the Marshal. He is clad in the light cavalry-style uniform common to his rank; note his fashionable cylindrical shako (later dubbed the 1812 model) and *à l'allemande*-pattern sabre. He wears *saroual*-style overalls common to troops serving in the Peninsula, where the climate demanded a loose-fitting and hard-wearing trouser.

*Plate F: Marshal Davout on the eve of Borodino, 7 September 1812*

Our illustration depicts the interior of the Emperor's field-tent; in the background, we can discern Napoleon's camp-bed, table, *escritoire*, lamp, folding-table and personal filing portfolio, all reproduced after the actual items he employed in the historic Russian campaign of 1812. Although Caulincourt (recalled from Russia in June 1811) had warned the Emperor of the difficulties of the climate, of the obstinacy of the Russians and of their intention to lure him into the vast interior by a defensive strategy, Napoleon was contemptuous of both the Tsar and the Russian people: 'Bah! A battle will dispose of the fine resolutions of your friend Alexander [the Tsar] and his fortifications of sand. He is false and feeble.' He therefore obstinately stuck to his plan for the morrow, to pin the Tsar's army down by direct frontal assault, while Davout vainly sought to impress upon him that the Semenovskoye redoubts, which he and Ney were supposed to seize, were more formidable obstacles than the Emperor seemed to understand. Davout's eye for economy could see nothing but a bloodbath, with precious little return, in this strategy; and instead he urged an outflanking movement of the Russian left which would cut them off from their capital and oblige them to quit their prepared positions. The victor of Austerlitz, however, would not risk this opportunity for a decisive battle and insisted upon fighting the Tsar's army on their own ground, feinting at their centre before seizing the key positions on their left, thereby exposing the Great Redoubt and Borodino itself.

*F1* shows Marshal Davout in a marshal's greatcoat. The Marshal shrugs in helplessness before the Emperor's stubborn determination to gamble everything on a decisive engagement. *F2* illustrates the Emperor Napoleon in his familiar grey greatcoat.

The end result was all that the meticulous and far-sighted Davout feared. The French casualties were 10,000 dead, 20,000 badly wounded, including the Marshal himself, 47 generals and 37 colonels. The gain was 2,000 metres of devastated countryside. The Russians, albeit with enormous casualties, retired on their capital and still presented a unified army.

*Plate G: Marshal Berthier at Imperial HQ, 1812–13*
The Imperial Headquarters (*Quartier-Général Impérial*) comprised both the Emperor's *Maison* (Household) and the *Quartier-Général* (Army Head-quarters) proper. As Chief of Staff and *Major-Général* of the *Grande Armée*, Berthier was in charge of the *Quartier-Général*, which consisted of the *Etat-Major* (General Staff) and the department of the *Intendant-Général* (Commisariat).

*G1* shows Marshal Berthier in campaign dress, 1812–13. We see the Marshal in a typical campaign situation, his headquarters a com-mandeered peasant's dwelling, the floor littered with the rough drafts of a score of different orders of the day to the many corps of the *Grande Armée*. At this period staff work was in its infancy, but the everyday logistic problems were enormous. Berthier's responsibilities lay not only in conveying the Emperor's orders to each and every unit of the army, but also in unearthing, collating and supplying every scrap of intelligence information concerning the enemy's army and country. Har-assed and overworked, it is understandable that he should write, 'I am being killed by hard work. A mere soldier is happier than I.' He wears the plain *frac* tunic, ornamented with the *plaque du grand-aigle* of the Legion of Honour and the aiguillettes of

*Général de Division* Grouchy, *Colonel-Général des Chasseurs à Cheval de la Garde,* 1809–14. He wears a plain dark green *habit* of light cavalry pattern, scarlet Hungarian breeches and dark green Hungarian boots, all richly embroidered with the lace of a *général de division*—one-third smaller than the marshals' pattern, but of identical design. Still some six years away from his baton, he wears the three clustered, silver, five-pointed stars of his rank on the tassels of his sash and epaulettes and integrated within the bastion loops of his breeches. His cloak is plain dark green, of the *manteau trois-quart* variety, and his scimitar's light cavalry-style swordbelt is crimson with gold ornamentation. (Feist. Courtesy De Gerlache de Gomery Collection)

*Major-Général* of the *Grande Armée*; behind him we can see his plain *redingote* hurriedly draped over the back of his chair.

*G2* is an *aide-de-camp* in campaign dress, 1813. Recorded from life in the Freyberg MS, this ADC wears the regulation dress, comprising a plain *Kinski*-style tunic and overalls in place of breeches and calf-length riding boots. Note the cut of the leather cuffs on his overalls, reminiscent of the contour of the Hungarian boots he would adopt in more formal circumstances.

Prince Poniatowski, 1809–13. As a light cavalryman foremost and a marshal second, this dashing Pole naturally wore his native light cavalry uniform, consisting of sky-blue *czapska*, dark blue *kourki* with crimson collar, and crimson trousers, the whole embellished with lace of Polish lancer officers' pattern. The Prince was only a marshal for three days and so never wore the standard staff officer uniform of the marshals. Although he entered French service in 1807, we can date this portrait from 1809, the year in which he received the Grand Eagle of the Legion of Honour, to which the *grand cordon* (sash) and the *plaque de grand-aigle* on his breast attest. (Contemporary engr. Author's Collection)

(A) The *plaque de grand-aigle* of the Legion of Honour. Although it frequently gives the impression of being all metal, in fact only the central device is so constructed; the arms of the cross and the rays between them are embroidery in silver thread. (B)(i) The marshals' baton was 50cm long, wrapped round in indigo velvet, embroidered with four rows of eight Imperial eagles in gold, and had solid gold ferrules; these were engraved with '*Terror belli. Decus pacis*' at top, and the particular marshal's first and second names followed by '. . . *nommé par l'Empereur Napoléon, maréchal de l'Empire, le 29 Floréal An XII*' at bottom. (B)(ii) Detail of the baton's Imperial eagle motif. The diameter of each eagle was to measure 4cm. (B)(iii) Ornamentation of the tops of the ferrules. (C) Hilt of the ceremonial sword awarded marshals-commanders-in-chief, 1812 regulations. (D) Ornament and buckle detail of senior staff officers' waistbelt. Marshals' pattern would comprise white leather belt with gold embroidery and a gold buckle. (E) Detail of tassel on marshals' sash. The two batons were stitched in dark blue and the ribbon in red. (Author's collection)

37

(A) Undress tunic showing lace disposition. (B) Ceremonial tunic. (C) Uniform button detail. (D) Epaulette detail. Again, the batons and ribbon are coloured indigo and red respectively. (E) Turnback device of all staff officers; marshals employed them solely on the undress *habit* and the *frac*. (Author's Collection)

$G_3$ is an *Adjutant-Commandant* in campaign dress, 1809–15. These important staff officers were appointed to every division of the *Grande Armée* to supervise and direct the day's march, billeting and feeding of the men and horses. They were also employed as assistant chiefs of staff to whole army corps. This individual wears a sober *surtout* tunic in place of the full dress *habit* illustrated in Plate B.

*Plate H: Marshal Ney at Waterloo, 18 June 1815*
Marshal Ney has been mercilessly castigated for his performance at both Quatre-Bras and Waterloo, yet it is doubtful whether he truly deserves the abuse so venomously poured on him in popular literature. Napoleon was a shrewd judge of the capacities and limitations of the men who served him, and it is squarely upon his shoulders that any blame must rest where a commander proved unequal to the circumstances that confront him. As we have seen, Napoleon did not cultivate men of initiative as subordinates, but instead sought agents to execute his own purpose without question. Among these were some exceptional leaders of men, of whom Ney must rank foremost, whose ability lay in commanding, cajoling, instructing, persuading, coercing or otherwise moving men to achieve the desired objective. Marshal Ney sought throughout the campaigns to be a leader by example, and he was true to that end in Belgium: he was a great field officer, not a staff planner. He did what was expected of him as such, no more, no less. We see him here towards sunset at Waterloo, having led the flower of the French cavalry to destruction on the British squares; having led the élite of the élite, the foot regiments of the Imperial Guard, to their doom in the face of disciplined volley firepower; and now with the *Armée du Nord* crumbling about him, trying to rally the pot-pourri of fleeing troops into some form of cohesion with his entreaty to the 95th Infantry: 'Come: I will show you how a Marshal of France dies!'

$H_1$ is a fusilier of the *95eme Régiment d'Infanterie de Ligne*, in the typical campaign dress of 1814–15. Despite the popular predeliction for unearthing the most colourful of the period's uniforms, the infantry of most armies more closely resembled this fellow: a sack of potatoes with a gun. Such was the rush to assemble the *Armée du Nord* that even the most illustrious of regiments were obliged to take the field ill-equipped and haphazardly dressed. The mass of infantry comprised youngsters and old men; the flower of the male population had already been expended in the course of the Revolutionary and Napoleonic wars.

$H_2$ shows Marshal Ney in undress uniform. The army was beaten physically and, more importantly, psychologically, through Napoleon's blatant attempt to dissemble the approaching Prussians as Grouchy's corps arriving in reinforcement. They had been betrayed. In his left hand we can discern the sabre the Marshal broke in frustration over a British cannon-barrel after unsuccessfully attempting to breach the bayonet-wall with cavalry.

$H_3$ is a trooper of the *1er Régiment de Cuirassiers*, in the service dress of 1815. The 1st Cuirassiers are known to have participated in the Belgian campaign without cuirasses. Doubtless dismounted in the course of the repeated charges at the British infantry, this veteran coolly reloads his *An IX*-pattern cavalry musketoon.

SOURCES
Cmndt. Bucquoy (Ed.), *Les Uniformes du 1er Empire*
Dr Hourtouille (Ed.), *Soldats et uniformes du 1er Empire*
H. Bouchot, *L'Epopée du costume militaire française*
Col. H. C. B. Rogers, *Napoleon's Army*
L. Rousselot, *L'Armée française*

J–C. Quennevat, *Atlas de la Grande Armée*
——, *Les vrais soldats de Napoleon*
R. Rudorff, *War to the Death*
P. Young, *Napoleon's Marshals*
Windrow/Mason, *Concise Dictionary of Military Biography*
H. Lachouque, *The Anatomy of Glory*

## Notes sur les planches en couleur

**A**  Murat à Eylau le 8 février 1807. Il porte un de ses uniformes moins prétentieux, une version blanche de la tenue réglementaire d'un maréchal, avec une culotte hongroise et des bottes, à la manière de la cavalerie légère. Il a avec lui son aide, le Capitaine Manhés; sous la pelisse il porte un dolman vermeil au col et aux manchettes jaunes, le tout galonné d'or.

**B**  Soult à La Corogne, du 16 au 18 janvier 1809. Il est en petite tenue, avec une cape. Son aide, **B2**, un capitaine de la cavalerie légère (éventuellement du 2ème Hussards) porte le brassard indiquant son grade d'aide de maréchal. **B3** est un Adjudant-Commandant en grande tenue—il s'agit d'un des officiers supérieurs affectés à chaque division comme chef d'état-major.

**C**  Masséna aux Lignes de Torres Vedras pendant l'hiver de 1810 à 1811. Le maréchal (**C2**) porte un simple frac comme tenue de campagne—les revers sont identiques à ceux de Suchet illustrés à la planche E. **C1** est un capitaine des Ingénieurs-Géographes, une branche des ingénieurs crées en 1809 pour assurer le service topographique et cartographique. **C3** est le fils et également l'aide de Masséna, le Compte Prosper d'Essling.

**D**  Lannes au siège de Saragosse, pendant l'hiver de 1808 à 1809. Lannes (**D2**) est en petite tenue à pied. **D1** est un officier du 1er Chevaux Légers Lanciers de la Légion de la Vistule, la formation qui avait fourni le noyau de la force de siège; elle comprenait quatre régiments d'infanterie en plus des lanciers. **D3** est un lieutenant d'une compagnie du centre du 1er Régiment d'Infanterie de la Légion.

**E**  Suchet tombe blessé à Sagonte, le 25 octobre 1811. Il porte le frac. Il est aidé par un sonneur de trompette de son fidèle 13ème Cuirassiers, portant la tenue type de la guerre d'Espagne, **E1**, pendant qu'un capitaine de l'infanterie légère, son aide, fait venir les infirmiers.

**F**  Davout se dispute avec son Empereur la veille de la bataille de Borodino, le 7 septembre 1812. Il porte la capote réglementaire d'un maréchal et Napoléon porte son manteau gris bien connu. Les détails du mobilier de la tente de l'Empereur sont authentiques.

**G**  Berthier travaillant dans une maison paysanne réquisitionnée pendant la campagne de 1812 à 1813. Il porte le frac, et les aiguillettes d'un major-général de la Grande Armée; sa redingote sans ornement est suspendue au dossier de sa chaise. **G2** est un aide-de-camp en tenue de campagne réglementaire, dessiné d'après des descriptions données dans le manuscrit de Freyberg par des témoins oculaires. Notez la coupe intéressante des manchettes de protection en cuir de son couvre-tout. **G3** est un Adjudant-Commandant, portant un surtout en guise de tenue de campagne.

**H**  Ney essaie de prévenir la déroute des Français la veille de la bataille de Waterloo le 18 juin 1815. Il est en petite tenue et serre dans sa main le sabre qu'il avait cassé sur un canon dans une crise de frustration. Le soldat de la 95ème Ligne qui est en fuite porte la tenue normale de campagne de l'infanterie de cette époque—un manteau difforme de couleur terne. Le dos de Ney est gardé par un troupier du 1er Cuirassiers, régiment dont on sait qu'il s'était battu à Waterloo sans cuirasses.

## Farbtafeln

**A**  Murat bei Eylau, 8. Februar 1807. Er trägt eine Uniform, die weniger übertrieben vorkommt als sonst bei ihm der Fall war: die vorschriftsmässige Feldmarschallsuniform, nur aus weissem Stoffe gemacht, mit ungarischen Reithosen und Stiefeln nach Art der leichtbewaffneten Kavallerie. Neben ihm steht sein Adjutant, Capitaine Manhés, der unter seinem pélisse einen hochroten dolman mit ledergelben Kragen und Ärmelaufschlägen und Goldtresse trägt.

**B**  Soult bei Corunna, 16.–18 Januar 1809. Er trägt petite tenue mit Umhang. Sein aide, **B2**, ein Hauptmann der leichtbewaffneten Kavallerie (vielleicht 2e Hussards?) trägt das Armband seines Feldmarschalladjutantenranges. **B3** stellt einen Adjutant-Commandant im Paradeanzug dar—der war einer der dienstälteren Stabsoffiziere, die zu jeder Divion als Generalstabschef zugewiesen wurden.

**C**  Masséna vor den Befestigungsanlagen zu Torres Vedras, Winter 1810–11. Der Feldmarschall (**C2**) trägt den einfachen frac als Feldanzug—die Aufschläge gleichen denen von Suchet in Abb. E. **C1** stellt einen Hauptmann der Ingénieurs-Géographes dar. Dieser im Jahre 1809 gegründete Abzweig der Pioniere wurde für Vermessungs- und kartografische Dienste erschaffen. **C3** stellt Massénas Sohn und Adjutant, Comte Prosper d'Essling, dar.

**D**  Lannes bei der Belagerung von Saragossa, Winter 1808–9. Lannes (**D2**) trägt das petite tenue à pied. **D1** stellt einen Offizier der 1er Chevaux-légers Lanciers der Légion de la Vistule dar. Diese Formation bildete den Kern der Belagerungskräfte und bestand aus vier Infanterieregimenten sowohl als den Lanzen. **D3** stellt einen Leutnant einer Füsilierkompagnie des 1er Régiment d'Infanterie der Legion Dar.

**E**  Suchet fällt verwundet bei Sagunto, 25. Oktober 1811. Er trägt den frac. Er wird von einem Trompeter seiner getreuen 13ème Cuirassiers geholfen, der den typischen Feldzug des Krieges in Spanien trägt, **E1**, derweil der aide, ein Hauptmann der leichtbewaffneten Kavallerie Sanitätssoldaten herbeiruft.

**F**  Davout diskütiert mit seinem Kaiser am Vorabend Borodinos, den 7. September 1812. Er trägt den vorschriftsmässigen Wintermantel eines Feldmarschalls, und Napoleon trägt seinen wohlbekannten grauen Mantel. Die Einzelheiten des Kaisers Zelt sind quellenmässig nachgeschildert.

**G**  Berthier bei der Arbeit in einem beschlagnahmten Bauernhaus während des Feldzuges von 1812–13. Er trägt den frac und die aiguillettes eines major-générals der Grande Armée; sein einfacher redingote hängt an seiner Stuhllehne. **G2** stellt einen aide-de-camp in vorschriftsmässigem Feldanzug dar—im Freyberg MS. geschildertem Feldanzug dar—bemerkenswert is der interessante Schnitt der Lederverstärkung seiner engen Beinkleider. **G3** stellt einen Adjutant-Commandant dar, der einen einfachen surtout als Feldanzug trägt.

**H**  Ney versucht die französische Flucht am Waterloo Abend, den 18. Juni 1815, anzuhalten. Er trägt seine Interimsuniform, und hält in der Hand den Säbel, den er in der Qual seiner Vereitelung über einen Kanonenrohr gebrochen hatte. Der fliehende Dienstpflichtiger der 95e Ligne trägt den normalen Infanteristen-feldanzug der Periode—einen formlosen, schmutzfärbigen Wintermantel. Neys Rücken wird von einem Reiter der 1er Cuirassiers geschützt. Bekanntermassen hat dieses Regiment bei Waterloo ohne ihrem Brustharnisch gekämpft.